THE ASSASSINATION OF
MARTIN LUTHER KING, JR.

THE ASSASSINATION OF MARTIN LUTHER KING, JR.

In 1968, severe racial tension gripped the United States. Great advances had been made by the civil rights movement during the previous decade, but now a so-called white backlash had developed, threatening further steps toward ending discrimination against black Americans. At the same time, the country was torn by protests over its involvement in the Vietnam War, while the national trauma following the assassination of President Kennedy in 1963 still was strongly felt. Amid all of these troubles, one man had come to be loved, and hated, as had few other men in American history—the Reverend Martin Luther King, Jr., widely considered the most inspiring leader black America had ever produced. Internationally known for his advocacy of nonviolent tactics as the best way to fight injustice, winner of the Nobel Peace Prize in 1964, King was visiting Memphis on April 4, 1968, seeking a peaceful solution to a labor dispute, when horrifying news flashed everywhere. The famous advocate of nonviolence had been assassinated.

PRINCIPALS

THE REVEREND MARTIN LUTHER KING, JR., the assassinated civil
    rights leader
THE REVEREND MARTIN LUTHER KING, SR., his father
CORETTA SCOTT KING, his wife

JAMES EARL RAY, the assassin
ERIC S. GALT ⎫
JOHN WILLARD ⎪
HARVEY LOWMYER ⎬ aliases used by Ray
PAUL BRIDGMAN ⎪
RAMON GEORGE SNEYD ⎭

ARTHUR HANES, SR. ⎫
PERCY FOREMAN ⎬ Ray's lawyers
HUGH STANTON, SR. ⎭

JAMES G. BEASLEY ⎫
ROBERT K. DWYER ⎬ prosecutors at Ray's trial
PHIL CANALE ⎭

W. PRESTON BATTLE, JR., judge at Ray's trial
ARTHUR F. FAQUIN, JR., judge at Ray's appeal

THE REVEREND ANDREW YOUNG, one of King's close associates
THE REVEREND RALPH ABERNATHY, King's main assistant
PRESIDENT JOHN F. KENNEDY, assassinated on November 22, 1963
PRESIDENT LYNDON B. JOHNSON, successor to Kennedy as President
PRESIDENT JIMMY CARTER, elected in 1976
SENATOR ROBERT F. KENNEDY, assassinated on June 5, 1968
RAMSEY CLARK, Attorney General of the United States in 1968
J. EDGAR HOOVER, longtime head of the Federal Bureau of Investigation

A FOCUS BOOK

THE ASSASSINATION OF MARTIN LUTHER KING, JR.

BY DORIS AND
HAROLD FABER

FRANKLIN WATTS | NEW YORK | LONDON | 1978

Cover design by Ginger Giles

Photographs courtesy of: Wide World Photos: pp. 3, 8, 17, 18, 22, 33; National Archives: pp. 23, 30; Norwegian Information Service: p. 27; Federal Bureau of Investigation: pp. 28, 46; United Press International: pp. 42, 52, 63; U.S. House of Representatives, D. O'Neill/K. Jewell: p. 70; George Mandus (photo by Ben Mandus): p. 74.

Library of Congress Cataloging in Publication Data

Faber, Doris, 1924–
   The assassination of Martin Luther King, Jr.

   (A Focus book)
   Bibliography: p.
   Includes index.
   SUMMARY: A biography of Dr. Martin Luther King, Jr., focusing on his involvement in the civil rights movement. Discusses the investigations of his assassination.
   1. King, Martin Luther—Juvenile literature. 2. King, Martin Luther—Assassination—Juvenile literature. 3. Baptists—Clergy—Biography—Juvenile literature. 4. Clergy—United States—Biography—Juvenile literature. [1. King, Martin Luther. 2. Civil rights workers. 3. Afro-Americans—Biography] I. Faber, Harold, joint author. II. Title.
E185.97.K5F3   323.4'092'4 [B] [92]   78–1726
ISBN 0–531–02465–2

CONTENTS

THE ASSASSINATION OF MARTIN LUTHER KING, JR.

ASSASSINATION

The shot that killed Martin Luther King, Jr., rang out shortly after 6 o'clock on the evening of April 4, 1968, in Memphis, Tennessee.

Not since the assassination of President John F. Kennedy in 1963 had the nation been so shocked. The second assassination of a major figure in the United States in less than five years raised basic questions about the character of the American people, the role of violence in American life, and whether there were evil forces behind the nation's political structure that would not hesitate to use assassination as a weapon to remove strong advocates of social change from the scene.

The question of conspiracy was raised from the very first minutes that the news flashed across the nation. It occurred to Ramsey Clark, the Attorney General of the United States, as he was informed of King's assassination. He telephoned President Lyndon B. Johnson, the man who had stepped into the presidency on the death of President Kennedy.

Put every available F.B.I. man on the case, the President ordered. So began the biggest manhunt in the history of the Federal Bureau of Investigation, aided by local police officers all over the world. Their first job was to find the assassin and their second was to run down all clues that would lead to others or to a conspiracy.

Clark set up a command post in the Justice Department Building in Washington, D.C. As reports about the crime and the search for the assassin began to flow in from F.B.I. agents on the scene in Memphis, they were overshadowed, however, by alarming news about rioting in the streets that came streaming in from all parts of the country.

In Memphis itself, rioters were shooting at police cars. In Washington, militant black youths rampaged through the streets, throwing rocks through store windows, setting fires, and looting. Raleigh, North Carolina, reported crowds out of control. In Harlem and in Brooklyn, gangs roamed the streets wildly. In Chicago, Pittsburgh, Baltimore—in almost every city with a large black population—thousands of men and women poured into the streets, some weeping, some bitter, some striking out in anger.

On that fateful night of April 4, it seemed that violence had triumphed over the forces of reason, that King's philosophy of non-violence had died with him. Not only was King dead by an assassin's bullet, but people were being shot and wounded in the streets. In Chicago, seven were killed and dozens wounded by gunfire. Other deaths and injuries occurred in Washington, Detroit, and Tallahassee.

In a nationwide television broadcast, President Johnson appealed for calm. "I ask every American citizen to reject the blind violence that has struck Dr. King, who lived by non-violence," he said.

*Martin Luther King, Jr., stands on the balcony of the
Memphis hotel, where he was assassinated the following day.*

But that was asking too much from the angry, sorrowing black community. Before the night was out the riots and violence had reached beyond the capacity of the police, and armed troops were called out to help restore order. A headline stretching across the front page of the *New York Times* the next morning summarized the situation:

ARMY TROOPS IN CAPITAL AS NEGROES RIOT;

GUARD SENT INTO CHICAGO, DETROIT, BOSTON;

JOHNSON ASKS A JOINT SESSION OF CONGRESS

As flags went to half-mast everywhere in the United States the day after the assassination, more Federal troops were dispatched to other cities, to Baltimore, Cincinnati, and Pittsburgh, to control looting and arson. Before the violence ended, 40 persons were dead and the toll of damage in 125 cities reached more than $30 million. It seemed as if America were undergoing an agonizing outpouring of hatred in reaction to the dreadful killing.

Yet King's creed of non-violence—despite the violence with which he was struck down—was remembered by most Americans. They stayed home watching the news of the manhunt on television or went to religious observances. They listened to his widow urging his followers to join in fulfilling his dream of a creative rather than a destructive way out of the nation's racial problems. In mourning, Mrs. King determined to carry on his work and millions of Americans made similar pledges.

"My husband often told the children that if a man had nothing that was worth dying for then he was not fit to live," she told a press conference. "He also said that it's not how long you live, but how well you live."

[4]

Even before the funeral, she flew to Memphis to lead a protest march that had been the reason her husband had gone there only a few days earlier. He had been asked by striking black garbage workers to help them in their fight for higher wages and union recognition. They knew his presence would dramatize their struggle as it had galvanized so many civil rights campaigns in the years before. Instead, his death transformed their routine labor dispute into an extraordinary national outpouring of emotion.

Mrs. King led a massive crowd of tens of thousands of people about a mile through the streets of Memphis to its city hall on the banks of the Mississippi River. It was an orderly and silent march, impressive in its dignity. Standing in a simple black dress of mourning against the white marble facade of the city hall, Mrs. King delivered her message:

"We must carry on because that is the way he would have wanted it," she said.

As she continued, her voice broke a little. "How many men must die before we can have a really true and peaceful society? How long will it take?"

That was the same question being asked in a different context by the public and the police. How long would it take to find King's assassin? That search went on quietly and methodically behind the scenes as the nation mourned the slain leader.

FREE AT LAST

It was a sleepless night for many all over the nation. The lights were on in the White House and in the Department of Justice Building in Washington. The rioting in the streets continued. Policemen and F.B.I. agents sped to their offices and then out again to trace down clues. A plane left Memphis carrying evidence to the F.B.I. laboratory in Washington. There Ramsey Clark decided to fly to Memphis. In Atlanta, Mrs. King prepared to fly to Memphis to bring her husband's body back home.

And in Memphis, after midnight, four black men drove up to the hospital where King had been pronounced dead. They were his closest associates, the Reverend Ralph Abernathy, the Reverend Andrew Young (who was later to become the United States Ambassador to the United Nations), the Reverend Bernard Lee, and the Reverend Jesse Jackson. They had come to pay their last respects to their slain leader.

An hour later, a black hearse carried the body of King through the streets of Memphis, now under a military curfew. No traffic moved except for police or military vehicles. Overhead a police helicopter circled, sending down a beam of light to search out movement in the streets below. The hearse went down

Union Avenue into famed Beale Street in the heart of the black district to a funeral home.

At about the same time, an emergency meeting got underway in Room 306 of the Lorraine Motel. It had been King's room. From that room, he had stepped outside to the balcony where he was shot only seven hours earlier. Now the chief lieutenants of the Southern Christian Leadership Conference were meeting without their chief to determine its future.

In King's chair was Ralph Abernathy. He and his colleagues decided they would go forward with a march on Washington to dramatize the Poor People's Campaign that had been King's last crusade. They also made plans for his funeral. King's body would be flown back to Atlanta in Senator Robert F. Kennedy's private plane. There would be a private service for the family and members of the organization at the Ebenezer Baptist Church, where his father was the minister. It would be followed by a public service later that day at Morehouse College.

In that room there were memories of King's last day in Memphis. He had made his last speech at the Masonic Temple there the night before. It was raining, but two thousand people had come to hear him talk about the strike of the garbage workers that had brought him to Memphis and about the march through the streets that they had planned.

King, in that speech, recalled an attempted assassination in New York in 1958, when a demented woman had stabbed him in the chest. "It came out in the *New York Times* the next morning that if I had sneezed I would have died," he said. "If I had sneezed, I wouldn't have been in Memphis to see a community rally around those brothers and sisters who are suffering. I am so happy I didn't sneeze."

*Ralph Abernathy (center) was one of King's closest
associates. They were both arrested in 1956
in connection with the Montgomery bus boycott.*

King paused. "We've got some difficult days ahead. But it doesn't matter with me now." In a fervor of oratory that held his audience spellbound, he continued:

"Like anybody I would like to live a long life. Longevity has its place. But I am not concerned about that now . . . I just want to do God's will. And He's allowed me to go up to the mountain. And I've looked over. And I've seen the Promised Land."

By now the audience was with him, emotionally moved, cheering, applauding, some with tears streaming down their faces.

"I may not get there with you, but I want you to know, tonight, that we as a people will get to the Promised Land." He paused again as the audience cheered and wept. "So I'm happy tonight. I'm not worried about anything. I'm not fearing any man."

He ended with words that plunged his followers into a tumult of emotion. "Mine eyes have seen the glory of the coming of the Lord."

It was as if he had a premonition of death.

A few days later, on Tuesday, April 9, a gleaming African mahogany coffin bearing his body was carried through the streets of Atlanta on a crude farm wagon pulled by two Georgia mules that were the symbols of his identification with the poor. It was followed by tens of thousands of mourners, black and white, the lowly and the powerful, who had come to pay tribute to him.

The affairs of the nation came to a halt as tens of millions of people all over the country dropped their work to watch the services on television. The cortege wound its way from the

Ebenezer Baptist Church to Morehouse College and then to the South View Cemetery where he was buried.

In a way, King preached the sermon at his own funeral. A tape was played of a service he had conducted only a few months earlier, and his voice and words rang throughout the nation:

"If any of you are around when I have to meet my day, I don't want a long funeral. And if you get somebody to deliver the eulogy, tell them not to talk too long.

"Tell them not to mention that I have a Nobel Peace Prize. That isn't important.

"Tell them not to mention that I have three or four hundred other awards. That's not important.

"Tell them not to mention where I went to school.

"I'd like somebody to mention that day, that Martin Luther King, Jr. tried to give his life to serving others.

"I'd like for somebody to say that day, that Martin Luther King, Jr. tried to love somebody.

"I want you to say that day, that I tried to be right on the war question. I want you to be able to say that day that I did try to feed the hungry.

"And I want you to be able to say on that day, that I did try in my life to clothe those who were naked.

"I want you to say on that day, that I did try in my life to visit those who were in prison.

"I want you to say that I tried to love and serve humanity."

And on his gravestone, they carved these words from an old Negro spiritual:

FREE AT LAST, FREE AT LAST

THANK GOD ALMIGHTY

I'M FREE AT LAST.

KING GOES TO MONTGOMERY

Martin Luther King, Jr. was born in 1929, the year the Great Depression started and millions of Americans were thrown out of work. He ended his formal education in 1954, the year the Supreme Court handed down its historic decision that segregation of the races in schools was unconstitutional. It was as if the calendar had set the twin themes of his life's work—jobs and equality for the black people of America.

In Atlanta, where he was born and raised, his father was a Baptist minister, a member of the Atlanta Voters League, and a trustee of Morehouse College, one of the leading black colleges in the country. More important to the growing boy, his father was unafraid—unafraid to speak out against segregation at a time when that was dangerous in the South.

As a boy, King had opportunities to see his father in action. Once when they went into a shoe store, they sat down in front, the place normally reserved for whites.

"If you will move to the back, I'll be glad to serve you," the clerk said politely.

"You wait on us here, or we won't buy any shoes," the father replied.

"I can't," said the clerk. They left without shoes.

On another occasion, when he was riding with his father, they were stopped by a policeman.

"Boy, show me your license," the policeman said to the elder King, using the traditional Southern way of talking to a black man then.

Angry, King replied: "Do you see this child here? He's a boy. I'm a man."

Silently, the policeman wrote out a ticket.

King never forgot those lessons from his father.

Even though he was growing up in the years when many families, black and white alike, had to scrimp to make ends meet, the King family was comfortable. Like many of his friends, King earned some money by delivering newspapers, but unlike them he spent his money on clothes. They called him "Tweed" because he was so well-dressed.

In those growing-up years, King was an active swimmer, tennis player, member of the neighborhood baseball and football teams, and a wrestler. But he was unusual in one way. Although he could take care of himself in a fight or a wrestling match, he preferred to defend himself by using big words. The other boys did not hold that against him; after all, he was a preacher's son.

By the early 1940s, when the United States was at war with Germany and Japan, the King family was prospering, even in a segregated society. It was a time when jobs became more plentiful for everybody, blacks as well as whites, in war industries, but it was still a time of segregation. Blacks served in the armed forces, but only in segregated units.

The pattern of segregation was universal. King went to a segregated school, but he didn't worry about it. He had found a new passion—public speaking and debating. He won the Elks Prize for a speech on the Negro and the Constitution. But what he remembered most vividly was the night the debating team returned to Atlanta from another city on a bus.

He and the other boys were forced to surrender their seats in the bus to white passengers—another custom in the South at the time. "It was a night I'll never forget," he said later. "I don't think I have ever been so angry in my life."

After graduating from high school at the age of fifteen in 1944, he entered Morehouse College, where his father had studied before him, with the intention of becoming a doctor. In his college days, King was solidly built, had charm, eloquence, an expressive baritone voice, and a great interest in pretty girls. But he soon found out that he wasn't suited for medicine, and decided to follow his father into the ministry. He entered the Crozer Theological Seminary in Chester, Pennsylvania, in 1948, a year when civil rights was becoming a major issue in politics.

It was a time when rebellion against segregation was stirring in the United States. Black veterans of the war were not satisfied with the old ways; they had served their country and wanted to be treated equally with white veterans. Black organizations like the National Association for the Advancement of Colored People were fighting segregation in the courts, with lawsuits contending that it was unconstitutional. Step by step, year by year, they won many cases, but progress was slow—and many blacks were impatient.

For King, however, philosophy and religion were his major interests. In addition to his Biblical studies, he became acquainted with Thoreau and his "Essay on Civil Disobedience" and the teachings of Mahatma Gandhi, who helped win independence for India through his practice of non-violent opposition to the colonial practices of Great Britain. King graduated at the top of his class at the seminary and went on to receive a doctorate in philosophy from Boston University.

While in Boston, he met Coretta Scott, who was studying voice. On their first date, he said to her: "You know, every Napoleon has his Waterloo. I'm like Napoleon. I'm at my Waterloo and I am on my knees." She was not amused, but he persisted and they were married on June 18, 1953.

A year later, King preached his first sermon in a church where he was the new pastor, the Dexter Avenue Baptist Church in Montgomery, Alabama. In the same month, in May of 1954, the Supreme Court issued its famous school desegregation decision, which raised the hopes of blacks all over the nation that the time had now come for real equality.

For the second time in the history of Montgomery, the man and the hour had come together. The first time had been back in 1861, when Jefferson Davis became president of the Confederate States of America at the beginning of the Civil War, which brought about the emancipation of the black slaves of the South. And now, almost a century later, another revolution—the black revolution for equal rights—was about to begin in Montgomery, with Martin Luther King as its leader.

THE BUS BOYCOTT

It started on a cold day in December. Mrs. Rosa Parks, a forty-two-year-old seamstress, got on a bus after a day of working and shopping. The bus was crowded, but she found a seat. In those days, the front of buses in Montgomery was reserved for whites and the back for blacks. At the next stop, the bus driver ordered Mrs. Parks to give up her seat to a white man. She refused. "I was plain tired and my feet hurt," she explained later. She was arrested.

The arrest triggered the famous Montgomery bus boycott that catapulted Martin Luther King, Jr., then twenty-six years old, to fame. Up to that time, he had not been connected with any of the black protest movements. Indeed, that was one of the reasons why all elements of the black community were able to unite and elect him president of the Montgomery Improvement Association to lead the boycott.

It is difficult to realize today how different conditions were then. Segregation was the rule in the South—in buses, at lunch counters, in washrooms, in department stores, and almost every public place—and it was rigidly enforced. The objectives of the bus boycotters seemed to be simple and reasonable—courteous treatment by bus drivers, passengers to be seated on a first-come, first-served basis, and blacks to be hired on predominantly black bus routes. But the city officials of Montgomery decided to "play it tough"; they would not bow to pressure.

Determined not to use the buses until their demands were won, the blacks organized car pools or they walked miles to work and back. One elderly woman sounded the call for all with these words: "It used to be that my soul was tired and my feet rested, now my feet's tired but my soul is rested."

But it was not easy. In January, King was arrested on a traffic charge, the first time he had ever been arrested, and jailed briefly. That did not stop him or his movement. Shortly after, his house, where his wife and baby were alone with a visitor, was bombed. An angry mob of blacks, armed with rocks, sticks, knives, and guns, gathered in front of the house in protest.

In anguish, King stepped in front of the crowd and calmed the hotheads with words that were to become a definition of his beliefs and the core of his leadership. "We must meet violence with non-violence," he said. King had spoken—and the crowd slowly dispersed, peacefully.

Feelings remained high in the community, however. King was arrested once more in March, charged with violating a state law against boycotts. He was fined $500, but he appealed. Meanwhile, in another legal action, four black women asked a Federal court to declare bus segregation unconstitutional.

The day King and Abernathy were arraigned in Montgomery, February 24, 1956, thousands of blacks protested.

By the end of *1956*, the bus boycott was over.

The court cases focused national attention on the boycott and its youthful leader. He was invited to speak at the Democratic National Convention that year. Leaders of national organizations came to Montgomery to see for themselves the new principles of non-violence in action. Day after day, week after week, month after month, the black working people of Montgomery continued to walk or use car pools.

Victory came in November—almost a year after the boycott started—when the United States Supreme Court ruled that Alabama's state and local laws requiring segregation on buses were unconstitutional.

At 6 o'clock one morning shortly thereafter, a city bus approached the stop near the King house. It halted. The bus driver smiled and said, "I believe you are Dr. King?"

"Yes."

"We are glad to have you with us this morning," the driver said.

The victory in Montgomery electrified the black struggle for civil rights throughout the country. The Southern Christian Leadership Conference was born, with King as its leader. *Time* magazine put him on its cover. King received the Spingarn Medal for contributions to race relations and was awarded the first of hundreds of honorary degrees.

But resistance to equal rights was stubborn. Some Americans, including J. Edgar Hoover, head of the Federal Bureau of Investigation, believed that King's movement was subversive. Some Southerners, including law enforcement officials, did everything in their power to stop the growing civil rights movement by arresting King and others.

One of these arrests, in 1960, affected the election of a new

President of the United States. In handcuffs, King was sentenced to four months of hard labor in a rural Georgia prison camp—a sentence that alarmed his family and the civil rights movement and aroused fears for his safety.

President Eisenhower refused to intervene. Vice-President Richard M. Nixon, the Republican candidate for President, declined to comment. But John F. Kennedy, the Democratic candidate, picked up the telephone and called Mrs. King, assuring her of his concern for her husband. His brother, Robert F. Kennedy, his campaign manager, called the judge and inquired about bail. As a result, King was released.

Those telephone calls were credited by political observers with changing the course of American history. King's father, a lifelong Republican, said he would vote for Kennedy. Enough black voters throughout the country did the same so that they swung the narrow election to Kennedy. Moreover, from that day on, the lives and the careers of King and the Kennedy brothers became meshed; so, too, were their deaths later on.

But the new Kennedy Administration did not change the face of segregation in the South. Black youths were arrested by the hundreds in sit-ins at lunch counters where they were demanding equal service. In 1961, black protesters began "freedom rides" to desegregate interstate buses and bus terminals.

King continued to lead peaceful demonstrations, squarely confronting the resistance of white merchants and public officials who believed that they could stop the rising tide of black demands by arresting him. King was willing to take the consequences of his actions, and was arrested once more in Montgomery and then in Albany, Georgia, and Birmingham, Alabama.

From a jail cell, he wrote his famous "Letter from a Birmingham Jail," a letter that explained the philosophical basis for what he was doing.

"I am in Birmingham because injustice is here," he wrote. "In the same way one should obey just laws, one has a moral responsibility to disobey unjust laws."

When he was released, he organized school children to march on Birmingham's city hall. They did, singing "We Shall Overcome." Hundreds of the children were arrested, but others kept on marching.

May 3, 1963, became an infamous date in the history of Alabama. On that day, police chief Eugene "Bull" Connor ordered fire hoses turned on the marching school children. As jets of water knocked the children down, the police loosed savage dogs to frighten them. But the police-state tactics backfired; a horrified nation saw the pictures and rose up in protest. Even policemen in Birmingham refused to follow orders.

King won the fight in Birmingham. President Kennedy said, "Bull Connor has done as much for civil rights as Abraham Lincoln."

Still, it was not easy. The resistance to civil rights continued. King organized a march on Washington to press for a new civil rights bill. A quarter of a million people responded and millions more, including President Kennedy, watched on television as King made what some believe was the greatest speech of his life.

"I have a dream," he said, "that one day on the red hills of Georgia, the sons of former slaves and the sons of former slave owners will be able to sit down at the table of brotherhood.

Martin Luther King, Jr., is again arrested in 1958, this time for "loitering"—a charge reflecting planned harassment.

*Martin Luther King, Jr., Robert Kennedy, and Vice-
President Lyndon Johnson at the White House in 1963,
five months before President John Kennedy was assassinated.*

"I have a dream that my four little children one day will live in a nation where they will not be judged by the color of their skin but by the content of their character."

In a masterpiece of oratory, he repeated the words, "I have a dream," as the mass audience cheered. He ended with a prediction that brought a hushed silence:

"When we allow freedom to ring from every town and hamlet, from every state and city, we will be able to speed up the day when all God's children, black men and white men, Jews and gentiles, Protestants and Catholics, will be able to join hands and sing in the words of the old Negro spiritual, 'Free at last, free at last, Great God Almighty, we are free at last.' "

It was 1963, a year of triumph and tragedy. On November 22, an assassin killed President Kennedy, plunging the nation into a despair that was matched only five years later when an assassin killed King.

THE NOBEL PRIZE

"How is the Nobel Prize winner for 1964 feeling this morning?" Mrs. King asked her husband. He was in a hospital in Atlanta for a medical checkup.

"What's that?" he asked.

"Martin, the Associated Press just called to tell us that the announcement has been made, and you are the winner."

As the news flashed around the world, messages of congratulations poured into Atlanta. The most famous international award had recognized the principle of non-violence, the foundation of the movement for civil rights that King led. King was proud and happy, but he realized that his work was far from done.

At a press conference in the hospital, King announced that the prize money, $54,000, would be divided among the various organizations battling for civil rights. Then, in December, the Kings, accompanied by their family and members of the movement, flew to Oslo for the ceremonies.

Uncomfortable in his formal striped trousers and gray tailcoat, the customary uniform for prize winners, King heard the citation read to the world:

"Dr. King has succeeded in keeping his followers to the principle of non-violence . . . without Dr. King's confirmed effectiveness of this principle, demonstrations and marches could easily have been violent and ended with the spilling of blood."

In his reply, King asked why the prize had been awarded to him. Then he answered his own question:

". . . I conclude that this award, which I receive on behalf of the movement, is a profound recognition that non-violence is the answer to the crucial political and racial questions of our time, the need for man to overcome oppression without resorting to violence."

Worldwide recognition of King and his movement did not mean acceptance by all back home, though. Not only did King have violent opposition among many whites in the South, but he had made a bitter enemy in Washington—J. Edgar Hoover, head of the Federal Bureau of Investigation. Hoover told a Congressional committee that he believed there was a Communist influence at work in King's organization.

That accusation stung King, who accused Hoover of aiding racists and right-wingers. Hoover stepped up the controversy by telling a group of Washington reporters that King was "the most notorious liar in the country." Although a truce in the war of words was soon declared, the F.B.I. began, according to an official investigation later, an illegal campaign to discredit King and destroy his leadership role in the movement.

Behind the scenes, the F.B.I. entered King's headquarters looking for documents that would harm him. They wiretapped his telephone and quietly made available to the press false and scurrilous information about him. All this was done, the Department of Justice report said later, despite the fact that King never

Martin Luther King, Jr., is shown here receiving the 1964 Nobel Peace Prize.

varied publicly or privately from his commitment to non-violence and never advocated the overthrow of the government by violence or subversion.

"To the contrary, he advocated an end to discrimination and disenfranchisement of minority groups, which the Constitution and the courts denounced in terms as strong as his," the official report said.

All this was to come out much later and cast doubt on the F.B.I.'s investigation of the King assassination, but its role in the surreptitious anti-King activities was not known at the time. To many Americans, white and black, King was a hero; to some, he was a disruptive influence.

Returning from Oslo, King had lunch with President Johnson at the White House. He used the occasion to advocate jobs and voting rights for the blacks of the South. But the interlude of prizes, adulation, and pleasant lunches soon ended.

The call was to Selma, in the heart of Alabama's black belt, so named because of the rich, black soil there. Few if any black citizens were registered to vote. They would stand for hours to register, only to see the registration desk closed when they reached the head of the line. Come back, they were told, but when they came back, they found the registration office closed.

In February of 1965, King and Abernathy led a peaceful protest march, but were once again arrested and jailed. When they got out, they organized another march of protest, from

*J. Edgar Hoover, director
of the F.B.I. until his death
in 1972, led anti-King
activities within the bureau.*

Martin Luther King, Jr., and President Johnson met often to discuss civil rights issues.

Selma to Montgomery, about fifty-four miles away. On Sunday, March 7, about five hundred men and women started the march on Highway 80, but King stayed behind, an action that was later to cause criticism. At the Edmund Pettus Bridge, the Alabama Highway Patrol stopped the marchers.

When they refused to turn back, state troopers wearing gas masks charged into the crowd, swinging clubs, throwing gas grenades, and using whips. A horrified nation watched on television.

King resolved to try again, and this time he would be with the marchers. His followers had risen to fifteen hundred now, black and white, and once more they marched to the bridge. Then they knelt in the roadway to pray as armed state troopers silently watched. Seeking to avoid bloodshed, King ordered the marchers to turn back—again drawing criticism from black militants who thought that he was giving up too easily.

Once again, white extremists broke the stalemate at Selma and gave the civil rights movement another victory by an atrocity that aroused the conscience of the nation. James Reeb, a white Unitarian minister from Boston, was murdered in Selma for no reason other than the fact that he was there supporting King.

On the evening of his funeral, President Johnson spoke to the nation on television. He compared the events in Selma to Lexington and Concord, where the American Revolution had started. Strongly supporting a new voting rights bill, he ended his speech by using the phrase that was the keynote of King's movement: "We shall overcome."

Two weeks later, King led still another march out of Selma, this time of five thousand persons, white and black. Under the protection of Army troops, they marched down Highway 80, across the now famous Edmund Pettus Bridge toward Montgomery.

But any thought that violence had been conquered was shattered by the news of another murder of a civil rights supporter. Mrs. Viola Liuzzo, a white woman from Detroit who had come to march, was shot and killed on Highway 80 while driving there.

The violence was not all on one side. Ten years after King had become involved in the civil rights movement with the guiding philosophy of non-violence, it seemed that violence was increasing—on the part of blacks as well as whites. Angry black youths, many of them unemployed, rioted in Watts, the black section of Los Angeles, and in Newark, New York, and Chicago.

King tried to channel the frustrations of jobless young blacks into his peaceful marches for freedom, but that wasn't enough for many impatient militants. They called him an "Uncle Tom," someone who refuses to fight for his rights. Some used the slogan "Black Power," believing that force was the only way to gain equality.

But King persisted—and expanded his campaign. He brought his movement to Northern cities and spoke out openly against the American involvement in the Vietnam War back in 1967, before most Americans did. Not only did he believe that the war was wrong on moral grounds, but he also said it was

Martin Luther King, Jr., leads a protest march in Selma. Andrew Young, now ambassador to the United Nations, precedes King.

taking billions of dollars that could be spent in a war against poverty at home.

Peace and freedom—King believed that they were inseparable. But now there was a division in the ranks of black leaders themselves. Some disagreed with his position on the Vietnam War. They believed it would hurt the civil rights movement.

Convinced that he was correct in opposing the war, King continued to speak out against it as well as condemning the rioting of black youths at home. But he knew that merely being against the rioting was not enough. What could be done?

Out of that search for a solution, King came up with the idea for a "Poor People's Campaign"—to give people jobs and hope instead of despair and anger. To dramatize the campaign, he would have a mule train—the symbol of the rural black poor —go from Mississippi to Washington. Thousands of poor blacks would camp in front of the Lincoln Memorial until Congress passed a bill providing jobs for the poor.

In the midst of his planning, he was interrupted by an urgent call for help—from Memphis, Tennessee.

THE LAST DAY

Back in 1968, Memphis was a city where blacks knew their places, working at dirty jobs for the lowest pay. Of all the dirty jobs in the city, none was worse than collecting garbage. The city's 1,300 sanitation men, almost all of them black, had no job security, no insurance, no facilities for washing, and no power. They had a union, Local 1733 of the American Federation of State, County, and Municipal Employees, but the city refused to recognize it.

In February, the union went on strike after its demands for a wage increase, a contract to meet their grievances, and a dues checkoff were refused. The black community supported the strikers, but the city was firm in its refusal to negotiate with the union. As the strike went on, a plan was adopted by the black union to bring national figures into Memphis to dramatize their cause. One of the leaders they wanted was King, who had helped so many other black struggles before.

The invitation came at a bad time for King, who was busy organizing his Poor People's Campaign. Reluctant to take time out for even one appearance, King finally yielded to the pleas of the Memphis strikers and spoke there on March 18.

"Why don't you come back and lead a big march here?" asked one of the strike leaders. Impressed by the large turnout for his speech, King agreed.

Unfortunately, the march that he led ten days later ended most unhappily. Unlike many of King's other ventures, this march was badly prepared and it disclosed a wide split in the black community between the leadership, which accepted King's credo of non-violence, and militant black youths.

The march started out mildly enough, with King and other leaders at the head singing "We Shall Overcome." At the rear, however, teenagers began to throw bricks and stones, break windows, and shout "Black Power, Black Power!" Before the day was out, 1 youth had been killed, 3 others wounded, 150 fires set, and more than 300 persons arrested. The National Guard was called out to end the violence. To many whites in Memphis and elsewhere, it was another piece of evidence proving that King was a troublemaker and the strikers irresponsible.

To King, the disruption of the march by militant black youths was most discouraging. It seemed that his version of progress toward equal rights by non-violence, which had worked in the past and brought him fame, was now threatened by unthinking young blacks. When an organization of black youths called "The Invaders" told him that the black people of the city were too worked up to carry out a peaceful march, King would not accept it. Despite the discouragement, he decided to lead another march; he would prove that non-violence was not dead.

On April 3, he returned to Memphis. He checked into Room 306 on the second floor of the Lorraine Motel on Mulberry Street. His aides were in nearby rooms.

From the balcony, to the left across the street was a fire-house, to the right the back of a rooming house. In the firehouse, two black detectives set up an observation post; they had orders to keep King under surveillance.

King had not asked for police protection anywhere, in Memphis or any other city. But Memphis was a city in ferment, with the National Guard keeping a lid on any further outbreaks, and King was a controversial figure. His life had been threatened a number of times. He had actually been stabbed once in an assassination attempt. But he had adopted a fatalistic attitude toward danger. He would go forward, whatever the danger.

The police of Memphis were concerned about the possible dangers to King, though, and it was their professional responsibility to keep order. Day and night, King was under guard. Forty men had been assigned to the King security detail, following him wherever he went, from his arrival at the airport to the motel, to the churches where he met with local black leaders.

In addition, the F.B.I., which had a continuing interest in King and his associates, had five paid informers providing information on what they called "the racial situation" in Memphis. They even had one undercover agent who had infiltrated into the leadership of The Invaders to keep them posted about what was going on.

The irony of these large-scale police and F.B.I. security plans was that they were unable to prevent King's assassination, but able to provide graphic and precise details of the last day of his life and of how the assassination was carried out.

King spent the entire day at the motel. In the morning, there were staff meetings on strategy for the march. Abernathy joined him for lunch—fried catfish. King visited with his brother in the early afternoon. At 4:30, Andrew Young came back from Federal Court where arguments had just ended on a Federal injunction to bar the protest march. After watching the early evening news, King returned to his own room to dress for dinner.

A few minutes before 6 o'clock, he walked out on the balcony and greeted friends who had come to go to dinner with him at the home of the Reverend Samuel B. Kyles, a local minister. In the courtyard below was a white Cadillac that had been put at his disposal while he was in Memphis. Standing beside it was the driver, Solomon Jones, Jr. Nearby were Andrew Young, the Reverend James Bevel, the Reverend Hosea Williams, and Chancey Eskridge, the lawyer who had argued in the injunction case.

"Solomon, start the car," King called out. "I'll be down in two minutes."

King returned to his room and put on his jacket. He came back out and leaned over the railing, waiting for his friend, Ralph Abernathy.

"It's getting cool out, Dr. King," Jones called up. "I think you'll need a coat."

"Okay," said King as he started to straighten out. It was his last word.

At that moment, a shot rang out. King fell backward. His jaw was shot away. His tie was snipped in two just below the knot. He lay in a pool of blood.

Abernathy rushed out of the room and leaned over him.

"Martin, Martin, this is Ralph," he said. "Do you hear me?"
There was no answer.

Others rushed to King's side. Young felt his pulse. He

thought he felt a tremor. Others hovered nearby as someone called an ambulance.

In seconds, police swarmed over the entire area. The ambulance came and King was carefully lifted up and sped to a hospital. But there was no hope for him.

Word of the assassination sped throughout the stunned nation. And the search for the assassin began.

MANHUNT

It was the biggest manhunt in the history of the nation. Before it was over, more than 3,500 agents of the F.B.I. and policemen all over the world were involved. They began to work within minutes after the shooting.

One policeman ran toward Main Street. In front of a store next to a rooming house, he saw a bundle covered with a dirty green bedsheet—with five inches of steel, the end of a rifle, sticking out.

"Did you see who put this down?" he asked a man who had just stepped out of the store.

"A white man . . . pretty well-dressed . . . no hat . . . dropped the stuff," the man said. He added that he had seen a white Mustang roar off within seconds after the bundle was dropped.

Seven minutes after the shooting, at 6:08 p.m., the police had their first firm clues as to the assassin. They broadcast this alarm:

YOUNG WHITE MALE, WELL DRESSED, RAN SOUTH
FROM 424 MAIN STREET. HAVE INFORMATION THAT
SUBJECT MAY BE IN A LATE MODEL WHITE MUSTANG.

[40]

Another policeman went into the rooming house.

"Did you hear a shot?" he asked.

One of the roomers replied, "A white man moved in today and I saw him run out after I heard a shot."

In a bathroom at the rear of the building, the police found scuff marks of shoes inside the bathtub and a palm print of a hand on the wall. Standing on the scuff marks, a policeman could look out the bathroom window and see the balcony of the Lorraine Motel and the door of the room King had occupied. It would have been an easy shot for anyone with a rifle.

Who had rented the room? The landlady looked at her receipt book. John Willard, she said. But who was John Willard?

And where was the white Mustang which witnesses said they had seen drive off? The car had disappeared and so had the killer. Was it good luck or careful planning by sophisticated conspirators?

There were no answers to these questions, but the investigators had better luck with the rifle that had been picked up in front of the rooming house. Through its serial number, they traced it to the Aeromarine Supply Company in Birmingham, Alabama. It had been sold on March 29 to a man who gave his name as Harvey Lowmyer. But who was Harvey Lowmyer?

At police headquarters in Memphis, the homicide squad went over the evidence they had found in that bundle together with the rifle. Most of it had been sent to the F.B.I. Crime Laboratory in Washington, but two items had been kept behind—a white T-shirt and a pair of shorts bearing the laundry mark 02B–6. Memphis police were checking every laundry in the city and F.B.I. agents were checking laundries throughout the country.

In addition, hundreds of F.B.I. men and police were out visiting every hotel, motel, and rooming house in the area, looking for traces of a white man with a white Mustang who might have stayed there the night before.

The questions were obvious. Were Willard and Lowmyer aliases? Were they the same man? Where was he? Where was the white Mustang? Above all, why was all that evidence dropped so conveniently under the noses of the police? Could it be a plot to mislead them?

None of the clues was made public, which led to a suspicion that the police were baffled. When asked about progress in finding the assassin, the police replied, "No comment." The F.B.I. was equally non-responsive. Ramsey Clark, the Attorney General, tried to still the public questioning. He said there was a large amount of evidence, that leads were being followed, and that there was no indication of a conspiracy.

"All of the evidence at this time indicates that it was a single person who committed this criminal act," he said. Reporters questioned that statement, made so soon after the crime and before the criminal had been found. But Clark was telling the truth. And the painstaking tracking down of all the bits of evidence brought results—only a week later.

In Los Angeles, the laundry mark was traced to the Home Service Laundry on Hollywood Boulevard. The manager said the mark 02B–6 had been assigned to an Eric S. Galt. Although

*Robert Kennedy marched
in the funeral procession
in Atlanta, Georgia.*

[43]

there was no trace of an Eric Galt, the police now had another name to work with.

Across the country, in Atlanta, a woman who had noticed a white Mustang parked near her house for several days called the police. The car was registered in the name of Eric S. Galt of Birmingham.

In Memphis itself, the check of the hotels and motels produced a registration for an Eric S. Galt with a white Mustang at the Rebel Motor Court on April 3, the day before the assassination.

But who was Eric S. Galt?

The F.B.I. Crime Laboratory ran tests on everything found in the car, in Room 5B of the rooming house in Memphis, and at the store where the rifle was bought. They determined that Galt was Harvey Lowmyer, the man who bought the rifle, and John Willard, who had rented the room in Memphis. A nationwide alarm for Galt was issued.

Meanwhile, F.B.I. agents were on the trail. They found that Galt had taken dancing lessons at the National Dance Studio in Long Beach, near Los Angeles, that he had registered in a locksmith course by mail, and that he had taken lessons at the International School of Bartending, also in Los Angeles. At the bartending school, they found a photograph of Galt. In the money orders sent to the locksmith school, they found two addresses—one in Montreal and the other in Atlanta.

At the Atlanta address, they searched his room. In a dresser drawer, they found a map with several places circled in pencil—King's home and the Ebenezer Baptist Church. It was clear they were on the track of the right man. More important, they found a fingerprint.

Two weeks after the killing, at 9:30 o'clock on the morning of April 18, the F.B.I. began the task of going through almost two hundred million fingerprints in their files to match the one they found in Atlanta. First they eliminated all women and men over fifty years old. Then they decided their first check would be of all white men under fifty wanted by the police—53,000 sets of prints.

It was a slow job. Twenty-four hours later, the F.B.I. agents had examined only 699 fingerprint cards. But on the seven hundredth card, they found prints that matched the one they had found in Atlanta. The card was that of James Earl Ray, a petty criminal who had escaped from the Missouri State Penitentiary in 1967.

"Galt and Ray are identical," J. Edgar Hoover announced. Ray's name was added to the list of the ten most wanted criminals in the United States.

The F.B.I. had identified their man. But where was he?

Although the clues were all carefully followed, he was not to be found. The trail was running cold and rumors of a conspiracy grew. Had fellow conspirators spirited him out of the country?

Once again, a bit of evidence turned up that put the police back on the trail. In Washington, an official of the American Southern African Council found in his files a letter inquiring about emigrating to Rhodesia signed by an Eric S. Galt. This raised the possibility that he had left the country. To do so, he would have needed a passport.

The F.B.I. had already been searching through passport applications without any luck. So had the Royal Canadian Mounted Police in Canada because of that Montreal address given to the locksmith school by Galt. Now the pace quickened.

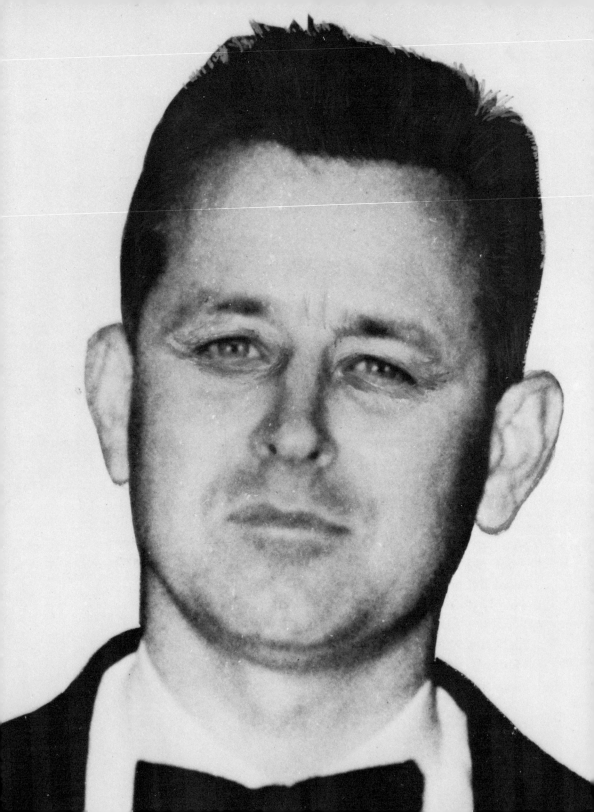

In Canada, a dozen searchers were going through about 200,000 passport applications filed since Ray had escaped from jail in 1967.

On May 20, a policeman found a photo that could be Ray's under the name of Ramon George Sneyd. Ironically, the real Sneyd turned out to be a policeman in Toronto. Under questioning, he remembered a curious story. Earlier that month, he told the Mounties, he had received a telephone call from a man who had inquired if he had lost his passport. The real Sneyd replied that he had not because he never had a passport.

From then on, the search for Ray was fairly routine. Checking the passport records of everyone who had left Canada, the Mounted Police found that a man using Sneyd's passport had left for London two weeks before and had not returned. In London, Scotland Yard alerted all airports to be on the alert for a "Sneyd."

On June 8, a man approached the desk at Heathrow Airport in London, with a ticket for Brussels, Belgium. He showed his passport. The police were called and questioned him. Then a police officer said formally:

"I believe your name is not Sneyd but James Earl Ray, also known as Eric Starvo Galt and other names, and that you are wanted in the United States for serious criminal offenses including murder in which a firearm was used."

Ray was silent.

And so, two months after King was assassinated, his alleged killer was in custody.

F.B.I. poster photograph
of James Earl Ray.

THE MYSTERIOUS "RAOUL"

From the beginning, it seemed incredible that a man like James Earl Ray could have conceived and executed the plan to assassinate King all by himself. It seemed even more astonishing that he could elude the police and escape to a foreign country without help.

A petty criminal, Ray had been in jail several times for robbery, but had never been involved in a crime where anyone was physically harmed. Why would a man like that murder King?

As the police and the F.B.I. went into his background, they found conflicting clues. He was about the same age as King, but his background was completely different. He was born in 1928 in Alton, Illinois, to a poor white family that others in the town called "white trash." His father, his uncle, and two of his brothers had been in jail. His mother became an alcoholic.

From the time he started school in the first grade, he was an outcast. His teacher said that he needed watching, that he was seldom if ever polite, and that he was "repulsive" in appearance. Even though his family considered him smart, he was left back in the first grade and had troubles throughout his school years. He never went to high school.

In 1944, when he was only sixteen, he got a job in a tannery. There he made a friend, an older German man who admired Adolf Hitler. According to one biographer, it was there that Ray became attracted to Nazis; to him, they seemed to be strong and to know how to deal with Jews and Negroes.

Two years later, after World War II ended, the eighteen-year-old Ray enlisted in the Army. He was sent to Germany at a time when cigarettes were very scarce there. Ray immediately became involved in black market activities. He didn't like what he saw in Germany—black soldiers mixing with white Germans, particularly white girls, and he began to drink heavily. He was court-martialed for drunkenness and thrown out of the Army. The Army said he did not possess the required adaptability for military life.

Back home, Ray turned to a career in crime. But he was an incompetent criminal, dropping clues about himself wherever he went. At one robbery, he lost his Army identification papers. At another, he got lost in a getaway car and returned to the scene of the crime. In a third, he robbed a United States Post Office and was quickly caught.

In 1960, after being caught just twenty minutes after he robbed a supermarket, he was sentenced to twenty years in the Missouri State Penitentiary. He became Prisoner No. 00416–J. Although he was not a successful criminal, he quickly learned how to conduct himself in jail. He got easy jobs and even made money by smuggling drugs and such to other prisoners. According to some of the other convicts, Ray was a loner and a racist in jail.

Like many other prisoners, Ray often talked about escape. But unlike the others, he did it. After failing in two attempts, he escaped in 1967 by hiding in a bread truck when it left the prison grounds.

From then on, he wandered across the United States and even visited Canada and Mexico. He got some money from his brothers, worked at odd jobs, and robbed food stores to get enough money to support himself on his travels.

In August of 1967, in Montreal, Ray said later, he met a mysterious underworld character named "Raoul." After engaging in some smuggling activities with "Raoul," Ray agreed to meet him later in Birmingham, Alabama. Ray said that "Raoul" never explained why.

On his return to the United States, Ray bought a second-hand white Mustang automobile for $1,995 in Birmingham and applied for a driver's license under the name of Galt. In that year and in early 1968, Ray enrolled in a correspondence course in locksmithing, moved to Los Angeles, took dancing lessons, visited a psychologist (to overcome shyness, the doctor said later), went to bartending school, and even had some plastic surgery done to change his appearance.

According to a reconstruction of Ray's activities made by the F.B.I. from its own and other investigations, this is what Ray did just before and on the day of the assassination:

March 29—Ray appeared at the Aeromarine Supply Company in Birmingham and bought a Remington rifle, using the name of Harvey Lowmyer.

March 30—He returned to the store and exchanged the rifle for a different one.

March 31—He rented a room in Atlanta, using the name of Eric S. Galt.

April 3—He went to Memphis, renting a room at the Rebel Motor Court, again using the name of Galt.

April 4, at 3:30 p.m.—He rented Room 5B in the rooming house at 422½ South Main Street in Memphis, just across from the Lorraine Motel, using the name of John Willard.

April 4, about 4 p.m.—He went down the street to the York Arms Company and bought a pair of binoculars for $41.55, again using the name of John Willard.

April 4, about 5 p.m.—He returned to the rooming house.

April 4, 6:01 p.m.—The shot that killed King was fired.

What happened then? How did Ray get away? Based on F.B.I. and other accounts, this is how he did it:

Ray drove his white Mustang south into Mississippi and then turned east into Georgia, arriving in Atlanta at about 6 o'clock the next morning, April 5. Just after noon, he took a bus to Cincinnati and arrived there at 1:30 a.m. on April 6. He went by bus to Detroit, then took a taxi across the border into Canada at about 10 o'clock in the morning and got on a train to Toronto, arriving there at 5 p.m. on April 6.

Despite the vast police network that was looking for the man in the white Mustang, Ray had no problem in getting away. Part of the reason was that he had left the car, and the police had not identified him as the assassin. His next step, getting a Canadian passport, was so ingenious that many observers were convinced that he must have had help.

On April 8, only four days after the assassination, Ray picked two names—Ramon George Sneyd and Paul Bridgman—from the birth announcements of newspapers for the year 1932, which he consulted in the public library. He then made the tele-

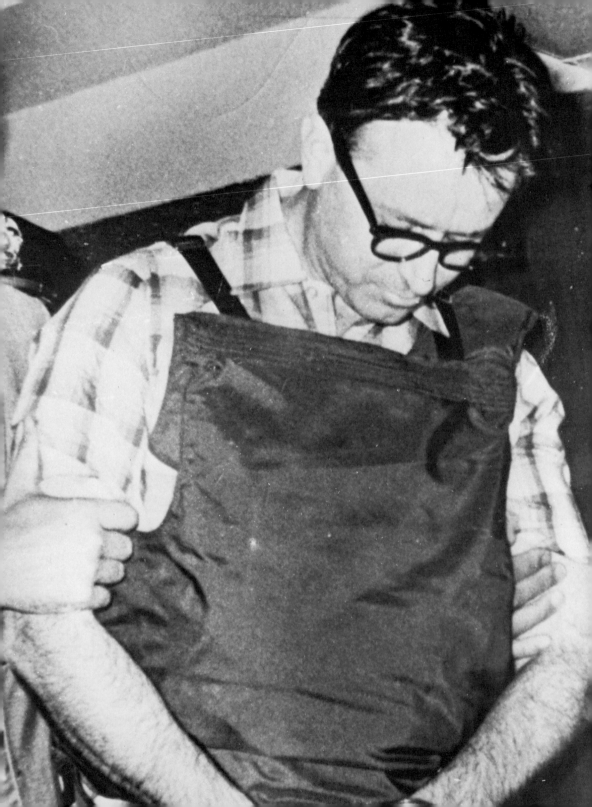

phone call that Sneyd remembered later. When he learned that Sneyd never had a passport, Ray asked for a duplicate birth certificate in Sneyd's name. When he got it, he applied for a passport in that name, and it was mailed to him on April 24.

Then came his flight overseas. After buying a round-trip ticket to London, Ray left on a British plane on May 6. From London, he flew to Lisbon, looking for passage to Angola, where he thought a potential white mercenary would be welcome. But he was unable to get there. He returned to London, where he once again tried without success to enlist in the mercenary forces fighting against blacks in Africa.

By this time it was June, and the United States was once again in mourning, shocked by the assassination of still another leader, Senator Robert F. Kennedy, brother of President Kennedy, now seeking the presidency himself. On June 5, Kennedy was shot and killed by an assassin in Los Angeles. Three days later, funeral ceremonies were held for the slain senator.

On that same June 8, across the Atlantic, James Earl Ray went to board a plane at Heathrow Airport in London. There vigilant agents of Scotland Yard arrested him.

Hardly more than two months after the King assassination the search for the suspected killer was over. But was Ray in fact the assassin? Did he act alone, or was he part of a conspiracy? Where did he get the money to flee the country?

Now the American people eagerly awaited the answers to these questions as the law began moving toward conducting a court trial of the accused man.

James Earl Ray is brought to jail after being secretly flown in from England.

[53]

THE TRIAL

By coincidence, it was Ray's forty-first birthday.

Escorted by two sheriffs, he appeared in the courtroom shortly after 9:30 on the morning of Monday, March 10, 1969. The chamber was packed with reporters. Armed deputies were on duty to make sure no attempt would be made to disrupt the proceedings. Ray's brothers, Jerry and John, were there too. The judge, W. Preston Battle, Jr., entered. The trial was about to begin.

Many in the courtroom, but few members of the public, knew that behind the scenes a series of meetings had been held among the lawyers. Ray's first lawyer, Arthur Hanes, Sr., of Birmingham, had entered a plea of not guilty to the charge of murdering King. At first, Hanes had thought he could convince a jury that there was a reasonable doubt that Ray had fired the fatal shot, but as he pursued his investigation he became less optimistic.

Every time he asked questions about "Raoul," who was the keystone of Ray's defense, Ray became evasive. After a series of disagreements, Ray dismissed Hanes as his lawyer and hired Percy Foreman, one of the best-known trial attorneys in the

South. The court appointed Hugh Stanton, Sr., the Shelby County public defender, to help him.

For the prosecution, the case had been prepared by three members of the state attorney general's office—James G. Beasley, Robert K. Dwyer, and the attorney general himself, Phil Canale. After examining all the evidence, they were convinced that Ray had committed the crime alone.

When Foreman began to go over the case, he too felt sure of Ray's guilt. As he cross-examined Ray in private about "Raoul," he became certain that it was a fabricated story.

The two defense lawyers tried to convince Ray to plead guilty to avoid what they thought was a certainty that he would be sentenced to the electric chair. Ray, however, said, "I don't want to plead guilty." He believed that no white man would ever get the chair in Tennessee for shooting a black man. Foreman convinced Ray that times had changed, that he could not deny the airtight evidence, and that if he pleaded guilty he could save his skin.

Would the prosecution accept a plea of guilty? The decision was up to Canale, who worried that if there were no trial, the public might believe something was being hidden.

He consulted the Department of Justice in Washington. Its advice was that since Tennessee allowed others to plead guilty, it would be inconsistent not to allow Ray the same right and might violate the principle of equal justice under the law. Canale also consulted Mrs. King's lawyer, who said that she and King's parents were morally opposed to capital punishment and would not object if he pleaded guilty and got a maximum jail sentence.

So in secrecy, Ray, his lawyers, and the prosecution, with the consent of the judge, reached an agreement.

[55]

On that Monday morning in March, Ray sat quietly in his seat in the courtroom as the proceedings got under way.

"May it please the court," Foreman began to speak.

Then he produced the bombshell. Ray was pleading guilty!

There would be no trial, no witnesses under cross-examination, no Ray under oath to tell his story.

"James Earl Ray, stand," Judge Battle said.

Ray rose.

"You are entering a plea of guilty in the first degree as charged in the indictment and you are compromising and settling your case on an agreed punishment of ninety-nine years in the state penitentiary. Is this what you want to do?"

"Yes, I do," Ray said.

"Are you pleading guilty of murder in the first degree in this case because you killed Dr. Martin Luther King under such circumstances as would make you legally guilty of murder in the first degree under the law as explained to you by your lawyers?"

"Yes, legally, yes," Ray said.

"Is this plea of guilty to murder in the first degree with an agreed punishment of ninety-nine years in the state penitentiary freely, voluntarily, and understandingly made and entered by you?"

"Yes, sir," Ray said.

Despite his guilty plea, under Tennessee law a jury still had to accept the agreed-upon verdict and sentence. Thirteen jurors —twelve men and one alternate—were quickly seated in the jury box.

The prosecutor began his presentation.

"Now there have been rumors that Mr. James Earl Ray was a dupe in this thing, or a fall guy, or a member of a conspiracy to kill Dr. Martin Luther King, Jr. I want to state to you as attorney general, that we have no proof other than Dr. King was killed by James Earl Ray and James Earl Ray alone—not in concert with anyone."

Canale said that his office had studied more than five thousand pages of evidence and three hundred pieces of physical evidence and had reached the conclusion that "we have no evidence that there was any conspiracy involved in any of this."

Foreman then rose to speak. He said his study of the evidence had convinced him that there was no conspiracy, just as Canale had stated and as Ramsey Clark, the Attorney General of the United States, and J. Edgar Hoover, head of the F.B.I., had stated earlier.

But then something unexpected happened. Ray stood up. "Your honor, I would like to say something, too, if I may."

With the court's permission, Ray said, "I don't want to change anything I have said, but I don't want to add anything to it either. The only thing I have to say is that I don't exactly accept the theories of Mr. Clark . . . and Mr. Hoover."

The court buzzed with excitement. Was Ray repudiating his confession? Was he saying there had been a conspiracy?

Foreman tried to explain. "I think what he is trying to say is that he doesn't think that Ramsey Clark's right or J. Edgar Hoover is right. I didn't argue them as evidence in the case. I simply stated that underwriting and backing up the opinions of General Canale, that they had made the same statement."

It obviously was confusing. Judge Battle asked Ray if he were changing his plea and his answers to the previous questions about his guilt.

"No, sir," Ray said.

To make sure, the judge repeated the question. "Are you pleading guilty to the murder of Dr. Martin Luther King in this case because you killed Dr. Martin Luther King?"

"Yes, sir, make me guilty on that," said Ray.

The prosecutor then introduced in evidence fifty-five statements of fact, signed by Ray. The most important of them was Fact No. 37, which read:

"That at approximately 6:01 p.m., April 4, 1968, defendant fired a shot from the second floor in the rooming house at 422½ South Main Street and fatally wounded Dr. Martin Luther King, Jr., who was standing on the balcony of the Lorraine Motel."

The statement of facts was important not only because it was a signed confession by Ray, but because it presented a chain of evidence that tied him conclusively to the crime. It started when he broke out of jail in 1967 and ended with his capture.

When the presentation was complete, Judge Battle said, "James Earl Ray, stand."

Ray stood in front of him, his head bowed, his hands clasped behind his back.

"On your plea of guilty to murder in the first degree as charged in the indictment, it is the judgment of the court that you be confined for ninety-nine years in the state penitentiary," the judge said.

But Judge Battle wasn't finished. "Why accept any plea? Why not try him for the electric chair?" the judge asked. He answered that all trends in the country were in the direction of doing away with capital punishment.

Then he raised the central question—was there a conspiracy?

"It has been established that the prosecution at this time is not in possession of enough evidence to indict anyone as a co-conspirator," he said. "Of course, this is not conclusive evidence that there was no conspiracy; it merely means that as of this time there is no sufficient evidence to make out a case of probable cause."

When the court adjourned, the case was not closed—despite the verdict and the sentence. A wave of outrage swept the nation because the question of conspiracy had not been fully explored in open court. One newspaper called acceptance of the plea of guilty "a shocking breach of faith with the American people, black and white."

And then Ray muddied the confused waters even further.

ESCAPE FROM JAIL

Three days after his trial, from his prison cell in the state penitentiary in Nashville, Ray wrote a letter to Judge Battle, denying everything. He said he was not guilty, that he had not killed King, that he had been pressured by his lawyer into pleading guilty, and that he wanted a new trial.

Two months later, there was a hearing on his request. The presiding judge was Arthur F. Faquin, Jr., a replacement for Judge Battle who had died of a heart attack. To Judge Faquin, the record was clear. Ray had voluntarily signed a confession and at that time had waived his rights to both an appeal and a new trial. He ruled against Ray.

But Ray was far from finished. In his cell, he had a typewriter, law books, a radio, a portable TV set, and the daily newspapers. For a man who had little formal education, Ray was an accomplished jailhouse lawyer—a prisoner who took advantage of all the legal openings he could find. He filed papers charging that his lawyer had forced him to plead guilty not because he was guilty in fact, but because the lawyer hoped to make a lot of money cooperating with a writer on a book and movie about the King assassination.

Ray came up with another explanation of what he had been doing at the moment King was shot, an alibi that he was to maintain steadfastly in the years to come. According to Ray, he had met "Raoul" at the rooming house, but had left before the shot was fired to get a tire fixed on his car. While driving around Memphis, his explanation went on, he heard the news of the assassination and left town.

Ray's changing story was unbelievable. It seemed clear that he was fabricating an alibi, but many who accepted Ray's confession in court that he had shot King still believed that the whole story was not yet told.

Ray now demonstrated his mastery of the use of prisoners' rights by appealing to the court that he was being subjected to cruel and unusual punishment, something forbidden by the United States Constitution. He said—and it was true—that he was being held in solitary confinement, alone in his prison cell, whereas the normal pattern of imprisonment was two men in a cell.

The reason was that prison officials were afraid that Ray might be killed if he were allowed to mix with the other prisoners, half of them black. Therefore, for his own protection, they kept him isolated. He cleverly turned that concern to his own advantage.

As a result, there was another court session in Nashville on December 29, 1969. This time, Ray took the stand under oath.

"Don't you know you're in jail because you killed a man who has a large following?" a lawyer asked him.

"I'm in jail because my lawyer sold me out," Ray replied.

Didn't he realize that many of his fellow prisoners might

want to kill him because of what he had done? the lawyer persisted.

"Then they should be locked up, not me," Ray said.

Ray won his plea. He was transferred to the Brushy Mountain Prison near Petros, Tennessee, where he became Prisoner No. 65477. A maximum-security prison in mountainous country, it was called escape-proof. Ray was put in a two-man cell in a wing with about twenty other prisoners who were unlikely to endanger him because of the King assassination. He was assigned to a job in the prison laundry and given the same yard privileges as other prisoners.

Meanwhile, the court proceedings on his plea for a new trial dragged on. He was turned down by every court he appealed to—by the Memphis court, by the State Court of Criminal Appeals, by the Supreme Court of Tennessee, by the United States Court of Appeals, and, finally, by the United States Supreme Court.

Their reasoning was simple. In the words of the Tennessee Supreme Court, "He made a bargain, swapping a guilty plea for a ninety-nine-year sentence rather than face a jury and a possibly harsher sentence. And now he must live with that bargain."

Ray had no plans to stay in prison, though. If he could not get out by legal means, he would get out in another way. In the years before, he had made so many attempts to escape that he had gained a nickname, "the Mole." He had escaped from the maximum-security prison in Missouri back in 1967. He determined to escape again.

Guards and bloodhounds tracked Ray when he escaped from a Tennessee prison in June 1977.

One night in 1971, he fabricated a dummy and left it on his bed, while he tried to escape through a steam tunnel. But it was 400 degrees in the tunnel and he was forced back and captured. A year later, he tried to cut a hole through the wooden ceiling of a room where other prisoners were watching a movie, but was captured again.

On his third attempt, on June 10, 1977, Ray succeeded in escaping. As the prisoners played horseshoes and volleyball in the prison yard, they were under observation by armed guards at seven of the eight watchtowers on the stone walls. Suddenly a fight broke out. Guards rushed to break it up. At the same time, mysteriously or by coincidence, a prison telephone system went dead.

In the confusion, seven men—including Ray—rushed to the wall near the vacant watchtower. They quickly put up a makeshift ladder made of iron pipes stolen from the prison's plumbing shop. They scrambled up and over the 14-foot-high wall and wriggled under a 2,300-volt electrified barbed wire that ran 18 inches above the wall.

A shot rang out. One prisoner fell. But the other six, including Ray, disappeared into the densely forested mountains around the prison. As the search began for the prisoners, with helicopters and bloodhounds, a skeptical America began to wonder once more about the uncanny ability of Ray to focus attention upon himself.

Although Ray was captured fifty-four hours after his escape, it was so well-executed that it revived the belief that he was a member of a conspiracy not only in his dramatic prison escape, but in the King assassination as well.

WAS THERE
A CONSPIRACY?

The American public was not satisfied with the simple solution to the assassination of King—not satisfied that Ray and Ray alone had killed him. Doubts were intensified by an outpouring of books, magazine and newspaper articles, and television shows about the case.

In almost every instance, independent reporters started their research on the theory that Ray was incapable of committing such a crime and escaping without outside help. By the time they finished, almost every one of the investigators became convinced that he had indeed done so.

Because of the persistent doubts and criticism of the F.B.I., the Department of Justice decided to review the agency's role in both the surveillance of King and the assassination investigation. It set up a task force that sorted through more than 200,000 documents and interviewed about 40 witnesses. Its verdict was anything but a whitewash.

It criticized the F.B.I. for its investigation of King for six years prior to his murder, although the evidence clearly showed that he was not a security risk in any way. It blamed J. Edgar

Hoover for illegal surveillance, break-ins, and wiretaps of King because of a personal feud that had no legitimate national security aspects.

Although it conceded the F.B.I.'s hostility toward King, the task force nevertheless concluded that the F.B.I. had conducted the assassination investigation "thoroughly, honestly, and successfully." Moreover, it agreed with the investigators who said there was no credible evidence of any conspiracy.

Yet, as one television commentator put it, the King assassination was "a case that would not be closed."

What is an objective observer to make of the persistent questions and doubts about the case? Here is a summary of the answers given in books, articles, and television shows, besides the Department of Justice report, the transcript of the trial, and media interviews with Ray himself:

Did Ray fire the shot that killed King?

He confessed that he did so in open court. The Department of Justice report called Ray's later assertion that he did not pull the trigger "wholly unbelievable" and intended as a ploy to reverse his conviction. There seems to be no doubt that Ray did in fact fire the shot that killed King.

Did he have a motive?

While in prison, Ray displayed a strong antagonism to blacks and the civil rights movement, according to many reports. The Justice Department said, "Ray stated that he would kill Dr. King if given the opportunity." Moreover, some of the studies indicated that Ray believed that sooner or later he would be treated as a hero in the South if he killed King.

In addition, one writer, William Bradford Huie, on the basis of letters from Ray, observed that Ray, a petty criminal, wanted to be "a big shot," to be on the F.B.I. list of the ten most wanted criminals. He achieved that goal.

Where did Ray get the money for his extensive travel?

This remains a puzzling question. The best estimate is that Ray spent about $7,000 between the time of his escape from jail in 1967 and his capture in 1968. The only verified income for him in that period was $664 earned by working in a restaurant for eight weeks. Where did the rest come from?

One writer said that Ray smuggled drugs into prison and sent a sufficient amount out—$4,600—to account for most of his expenses. Another investigator said Ray committed several hold-ups to raise money. The F.B.I. reported that his brothers gave him some money. Ray himself said the money came from "Raoul."

After an exhaustive study, the F.B.I. admitted that "the sources for Ray's funds still remain a mystery today." The answer could be a combination of the above—some money from smuggling, some from working, some from robbery, and some from his brothers.

Why were two black police officers removed from their observation of King just before the assassination?

The Memphis Police Department had assigned Edward R. Reditt and Willie B. Richmond to keep King under surveillance while he was in the city. They posted themselves in the rear of the fire station where they could observe King and his associates at the Lorraine Motel. At 4 p.m. on April 4, two hours before the assassination, Reditt was recalled to headquarters, where he was told he was being sent home because of a telephone threat on his life. Richmond remained. It was Richmond who telephoned headquarters at 6:01 p.m. to report that King had been shot.

Although the Reditt recall was suspiciously coincidental—and became a key element in a book by Mark Lane alleging a conspiracy to kill King—it is difficult to see how this could have been part of a plot against King. Richmond remained at the firehouse, which was an observation post, not a place from which King could have been protected. There was nothing that Richmond alone or Richmond and Reditt together could have done to prevent the assassination. As for catching the assassin, there were dozens of other policemen in the immediate vicinity.

Was there a "Raoul"?

To Ray, "Raoul" was the man who sent him to Memphis. On one television interview, Ray described Raoul as a Latin, about 5'5", weighing 150 pounds, with auburn hair. Ray told interviewers that Raoul was in the rooming house when the shot was fired and that he himself was not.

No one has ever found a trace of "Raoul" outside of Ray's statements. To most observers, "Raoul" is a fictitious character created by Ray to explain his presence in Memphis and to back up his claim that he did not kill King. It is an unbelievable story.

Were others involved?

There is no evidence at all that anyone helped Ray in the assassination. There is evidence that his brothers, Jerry and John, helped Ray after his escape from jail and after he fled from Memphis.

Was there a conspiracy?

No evidence to date has been found to support the theory that there was a conspiracy to murder King. There have been suspicions and doubts about the story of Ray's life and King's death. It seemed too simple to be true—that one man who hated blacks could have performed the evil deed alone. Yet almost every independent investigator has become convinced that Ray did so.

Police officers know that in any criminal investigation it is impossible to prove conclusively that others besides the culprit might *not* be involved in a crime. That poses a problem for people who want all their doubts resolved, not just the reasonable doubts that a jury must overcome to convict a man of a crime, even of murder.

Here is how the Department of Justice task force summed up that aspect of the case:

"We acknowledge that proof of the negative, i.e., proof that others were not involved, is here as elusive and difficult as it has universally been in criminal law. But the sum of all the evidence of Ray's guilt points to him so exclusively that it most effectively makes the point that no one else was involved. Of course, someone could conceivably have provided him with logistics, or even paid him to commit the crime. However, we have found no competent evidence upon which to base such a theory."

That left a loophole—was it possible that someone did pay Ray to murder King?

And another question arose. Why should Americans accept the conclusions of a Department of Justice inquiry into one of its own subordinate agencies? In the post-Watergate climate of skepticism, that question was valid. Some black leaders said that only a Congressional committee could come up with answers that the public would accept.

As a result, in 1976 a House of Representatives Select Committee was appointed to investigate the assassinations of both King and President Kennedy. But the first reports from inside that committee indicated that almost all of the new leads that it followed had been gone over before and that almost all of the rumored "new" information it uncovered had already been sifted.

Perhaps the simple explanation was true—that there had been no conspiracy and that Ray and Ray alone had murdered King.

*Louis Stokes is chairman
of the House committee
investigating the King
and Kennedy assassinations.*

[71]

AFTERMATH

One of the dreams of Martin Luther King, Jr. came true in 1976, the year America celebrated its bicentennial. A white man from Georgia, Jimmy Carter, was elected President of the United States, with the help of a black man from Georgia, Andrew Young, who had been standing by King's side when he was shot.

When Carter took the oath of office as President, the nation was at peace again. No soldiers, black or white, fought and died in Vietnam as they had in the years during which King had opposed the war. Although King's dream of true equality at home was far from reached, his legacy of non-violence dominated the continuing struggle for jobs and for housing and school integration in both the North and the South. Even the black power militants seemed to accept the principle that progress would be made through education, negotiation, and lawsuit, not by rioting in the streets.

King's memory was kept alive in other ways, too. Ironically, it was Ray, his assassin, who periodically revived the case with press interviews. His comments fell into a pattern of denying that he had shot King, and asserting it was all his lawyer's fault that he had pleaded guilty.

But the memory of King's life and contributions over-shadowed the lingering doubts about his death. His birthday—January 15—became a holiday in many states and his name became a symbol of the struggle for racial justice.

Nine years after King's death, in 1977, President Carter recognized his unique contributions to all Americans. He awarded the nation's highest honor, the Presidential Medal of Freedom, to Martin Luther King, Jr., because of the truths that he had spoken and struggled for.

In presenting the medal to King's widow and father, President Carter summed up his accomplishments:

"Martin Luther King, Jr., was the conscience of his generation. A Southerner, a black man, he gazed on the great wall of segregation and saw that the power of love could bring it down.

"From the pain and exhaustion of his fight to free all people from the bondage of separation and injustice, he wrung eloquent statement of his dreams of what America could be.

"He helped us overcome our ignorance of each other. He spoke out against a war he felt was unjust as he had spoken out against laws that were unfair.

"He made our nation stronger because he made it better. Honored by kings, he continued in his last days to strive for a world where the poorest and humblest among us could enjoy the fulfillment of the promises of our founding fathers.

"His life informed us, his dreams sustain us yet."

Martin Luther King's truths go marching on today, but his life and death are not a fictitious mystery story. It has been proved beyond a reasonable doubt that James Earl Ray alone

killed King. No one has come up with any credible evidence that there was a conspiracy. From time to time, someone may offer a new theory for those who are not satisfied with Ray's conviction. As a result, there can be no final chapter to tidy up all the loose ends and answer all the unanswered questions to everyone's satisfaction.

President Jimmy Carter
was, and is, a great admirer of
Martin Luther King, Jr.

A SELECTED BIBLIOGRAPHY

Bennett, Lerone, Jr. *What Manner of Man?* Chicago: Johnson, 1968.

Frank, Gerold. *An American Death*. New York: Doubleday, 1972.

Huie, William Bradford. *He Slew the Dreamer*. New York: Delacorte, 1968.

King, Coretta Scott. *My Life with Martin Luther King, Jr.* New York: Holt, Rinehart and Winston, 1969.

Lane, Mark, and Gregory, Dick. *Code Name Zorro*. Englewood Cliffs, N.J.: Prentice-Hall, 1977.

Lewis, David L. *King: A Critical Biography*. New York: Praeger, 1970.

McMillan, George. *The Making of an Assassin: The Life of James Earl Ray*. Boston: Little, Brown, 1976.

Report of the Department of Justice Task Force to Review the F.B.I. Martin Luther King, Jr. Security and Assassination Investigations. Washington, D.C.: Department of Justice, 1977.

INDEX